Potatoes
with a twist

igloobooks

igloobooks

Published in 2013
by Igloo Books Ltd
Cottage Farm
Sywell
NN6 0BJ
www.igloobooks.com

Food photography and recipe development: PhotoCuisine UK
Front and back cover images © PhotoCuisine UK

HUN001 0813
2 4 6 8 10 9 7 5 3 1
ISBN 978-1-78197-433-9

Printed and manufactured in China

Potatoes
with a twist

Contents

Light Bites and Lunches

Salmon and Sweet Potato Timbales

Serves: **4** Preparation time: **15 minutes** Cooking time: **15 minutes**

Ingredients

3 large sweet potatoes, peeled

salt and pepper

50 g / 1 ¾ oz butter

400 g / 14 oz / 1 ½ cups cooked flaked salmon

¼ bunch chervil finely chopped

80 g / 2 ½ oz / ⅓ cup Cheddar cheese, grated

Method

Cut the potatoes into large chunks and cook in boiling salted water until tender – about 10-12 minutes.

Drain thoroughly, then set the pan over a low heat and shake the pan to drive off any excess moisture. Mash thoroughly with the butter until smooth then season generously.

Carefully fold the salmon flakes and herbs through the potato, trying to keep the salmon as whole as possible.

Spoon equal amounts into ring moulds on serving plates and top with a little grated Cheddar cheese. Grill until the cheese is bubbling and serve.

Tartiflette Sandwiches

Serves: **4** Preparation time: **20 minutes** Cooking time: **5-10 minutes**

Ingredients

8 waxy potatoes

4 thick slices of
bread, toasted

100 g / 3 ½ oz / ½ cup
quark cheese
(low-fat soft cheese)

4 thick slices of ham

2 tbsp butter, melted

salt and pepper

200 g / 7 oz / ¾ cup
strong Cheddar or
Gruyère cheese, shaved

Method

Slice the potatoes about the thickness of 5 mm / 0.5 cm and
steam over simmering water until completely tender. Drain
briefly on kitchen paper.

Spread the toast with the quark cheese and lay a slice of ham
on top.

Divide the potato slices equally and lay them like fish scales
or roof tiles over the ham, overlapping the rows slightly.

Brush with melted butter, season and top with shavings
of cheese.

Grill on a foil-lined tray until the cheese is bubbling. Serve hot.

Potato Pumpkin Rosti with Goats' Cheese

Serves: **4** Preparation time: **20 minutes** Cooking time: **20 minutes**

Ingredients

250 g / 9 oz / 1 cup
floury potatoes, peeled

250 g / 9 oz / 1 cup
butternut squash,
peeled, halved and
seeded

2 tbsp butter, melted

80 ml / 2 ½ fl. oz /
⅓ cup vegetable oil

salt and pepper

4 thick slices
goats' cheese

4 sprigs chervil

Method

Grate the potatoes and squash. Toss with the melted butter and seasoning, ensuring they are thoroughly coated.

Heat the oil in a large frying pan, then add the mixture to the pan using a large tablespoon for each portion, flattening it slightly with a spatula. Cook over a medium heat for about 10 minutes until the base is brown.

Run the spatula or a palette knife underneath to loosen, then turn each rosti over to cook on the other side. Cook for a further 10 minutes until browned and crisp.

Drain briefly on kitchen paper then top with a slice of goats' cheese and chervil before serving.

Sweet Potato Chips with Broccoli Dip

Serves: **6-8** Preparation time: **20 minutes** Cooking time: **10 minutes**

Ingredients

450 g / 1 lb / 2 cups
sweet potatoes, peeled

1 L / 2 ¼ pints / 4 ¼
cups vegetable oil

salt

For the dip:

1 head of broccoli,
broken into florets

50 g / 2 oz blue
cheese, crumbled

200-250 ml / 7-9 fl. oz /
¾ - 1 cup sour cream

1 tbsp extra virgin
olive oil

Method

To make the dip, steam the broccoli florets until tender, then tip into a food processor. Add the cheese and some of the sour cream and blitz to a puree - you may need to add more cream, but keep tasting. Drizzle in the oil, season and set aside.

Slice the potatoes as thin as you can, either using a mandoline or a very sharp knife. Wash in cold water to get rid of the starch.

Heat the oil until a cube of bread sizzles immediately when dropped in, then fry the potatoes in batches until golden.

Remove to kitchen paper to drain and sprinkle liberally with salt, then serve with the dip.

14

Crisp Curried Potato Parcels

Serves: **6** Preparation time: **35 minutes** Cooking time: **20-25 minutes**

Ingredients

6 potatoes, peeled

2 bunches coriander (cilantro), chopped

2 tsp curry powder or garam masala

salt and pepper

24 sheets of filo pastry

70 g / 2 ½ oz / ⅓ cup butter, melted

Method

Preheat the oven to 200°C (180° fan) / 400F / gas 6.

Cook the potatoes in boiling salted water for about 25 minutes or until tender to the point of a knife. Drain.

Roughly crush the potatoes. Add the coriander, curry powder then season and mix well.

Lay out the filo pastry sheets and brush with melted butter. Using two sheets at a time, lay them out on the work surface, place a large tbsp of potato mixture in the centre and fold to form a rectangle, sealing the edges with a little melted butter. Repeat until all the sheets and mixture are used up.

Place on a baking tray and bake for 20-25 minutes until crisp and golden. You may need to turn them halfway through cooking.

Serve with a spicy sauce or plain yoghurt on the side.

Duchesse Potatoes with Almonds

Serves: **4-6** Preparation time: **30 minutes** Cooking time: **15 minutes**

Ingredients

1.5 kg / 3 lb / 6 cups potatoes, peeled and cut into chunks

150 ml / 5 fl. oz / ⅔ cup milk

100 g / 3 ½ oz / ½ cup butter

3 eggs, beaten

salt and pepper

150 g / 5 oz / ⅔ cup flaked (slivered) almonds

Method

Preheat the oven to 220°C (200° fan) / 425F / gas 7.

Cook the potatoes in boiling salted water until tender to the point of a knife. Drain thoroughly and return briefly to the heat to drive off any excess water.

Mash the potatoes thoroughly with a potato ricer or hand-held masher.

Heat the milk and butter until the butter has melted, then stir into the potatoes with 2 of the beaten eggs and season to taste.

Spoon the mixture into a piping bag with a 1.25 cm / ½ inch star nozzle and pipe into pyramid shapes onto a greased baking tray. Brush with the remaining egg and sprinkle on the almonds, patting them on to help them stick.

Bake in the oven for 15 minutes or until golden. Serve immediately.

Potato and Pickled Herring Brochettes

Serves: **4** Preparation time: **10 minutes** Cooking time: **15 minutes**

Ingredients

2 large floury potatoes, peeled

extra virgin olive oil

salt and pepper

250 g / 9 oz / 1 cup marinated rollmop herrings, drained

2 shallots, finely chopped

¼ bunch parsley, finely chopped

Method

Cut the potatoes into chunks and steam over simmering water until tender to the point of a knife.

When cooked, toss with 2 tbsp extra virgin olive oil and season.

Thread onto skewers, alternating with chunks of herring.

Sprinkle over shallots and parsley and serve.

Potato, Goats' Cheese and Coriander Frittata

Serves: **6** Preparation time: **10 minutes** Cooking time: **35 minutes**

Ingredients

2 large floury potatoes, peeled and diced

8 eggs

1 tbsp crème fraîche

100 g / 3 ½ oz / ½ cup goats' cheese, cubed

½ bunch coriander (cilantro), chopped

olive oil

salt and pepper

2 very ripe avocados, halved and stoned

1 lime, juiced

1 tsp sesame oil

Method

Preheat the oven to 180°C (160° fan) / 350F / gas 4.

Steam the potatoes over simmering water for about 5-7 minutes until tender to the point of a knife.

Beat the eggs with the crème fraîche in a large bowl.

Add the potatoes, cheese and coriander. Season, then mix together carefully.

Oil a large frying pan, then pour the mixture in and bake in the oven for about 35 minutes until puffed and golden. The egg should be cooked through.

Meanwhile mash the avocado flesh roughly with lime juice and sesame oil. Season well.

Cut the frittata into wedges and serve warm or cold.

Potato and Parsley Samosas

Serves: **6** Preparation time: **25 minutes** Cooking time: **15 minutes**

Ingredients

24 sheets of filo pastry

6 potatoes, peeled

2 bunches parsley, chopped

2 tsp curry powder

1-2 limes, juiced

salt

70 g / 2 ½ oz / ⅓ cup butter, melted

oil for deep frying

Method

Cook the potatoes in boiling salted water for about 25 minutes or until tender to the point of a knife. Drain.

Roughly crush the potatoes. Add the parsley, curry powder and lime juice. Salt and mix well.

Lay out the filo pastry and brush with melted butter. Using two sheets at a time, lay them on the work surface, place a large tbsp of potato mixture in the centre and fold to form a triangle. Repeat until all the sheets and mixture are used up.

Heat the oil, then add the samosas carefully, two at a time. Cook until they are golden and crisp on both sides, then remove to kitchen paper.

Serve with a spicy sauce or plain yoghurt on the side.

Sweet Potato Soup

Serves: **4**   Preparation time: **10 minutes**   Cooking time: **40 minutes**

Ingredients

30 g / 1 oz butter

1 onion

2 garlic cloves, sliced

500 g / 1 lb / 2 cups sweet potatoes

2 sprigs thyme

1 tsp garam masala

pinch of dried chilli (chili) flakes

1 L / 2 ¼ pints / 4 ¼ cups chicken stock

8 raw shelled prawns

salt and pepper

100 ml / 3 ½ fl. oz / ½ cup single (light) cream

Method

Sweat the peeled and sliced onion and garlic in the butter in a large pan, until golden and soft.

Peel the potatoes and cut into chunks, then add the potatoes to the pan and cook for five minutes. Next add the thyme, spices and stock.

Simmer for about 20 minutes or until the potatoes are tender.

Allow to cool a little, remove the thyme stems then blitz in a food processor or with a hand-held blender until smooth.

Reheat and add the prawns, simmering for 5 minutes until they turn pink.

Season and stir in the cream, reheating gently.

26

Potato and Bacon Omelette Rolls

Serves: **4**   Preparation time: **15 minutes**   Cooking time: **20-30 minutes**

Ingredients

250 g / 9 oz / 1 cup potatoes, peeled and diced

30 g / 1 oz butter

4 rashers smoked streaky bacon, diced

salt and pepper

2 tbsp parsley, chopped

30 g / 1 oz butter

8 eggs

Method

Cook the potatoes for 5 minutes in boiling salted water until tender. Drain thoroughly and set aside in a bowl.

Heat the butter in a pan and fry the bacon until golden and crisp then tip into the potatoes, stir in the parsley and season.

Meanwhile crack 2 of the eggs into a bowl and beat lightly. Heat the butter in the pan, add the eggs and swirl gently to cover the base of the pan and help it set.

When the omelette is nearly set, spoon in the potato mixture and use a spatula to roll the omelette up around the filling.

Remove from the pan and place in the oven on a low heat while you repeat with the remaining eggs and potato mixture.

Serve warm with light soy sauce or a dressing of your choice.

Chickpea and Sweet Potato Fritters

Serves: **4**   Preparation time: **15 minutes**   Cooking time: **15-20 minutes**

Ingredients

2 large sweet potatoes, peeled

1 onion, peeled and chopped

400 g / 14 oz / 1½ cups canned chickpeas (garbanzo beans), drained

2 cloves of garlic, chopped

salt and pepper

3 tbsp olive oil

100 g / 3 ½ oz / ½ cup pistachios, chopped

Method

Grate the sweet potatoes then tip into a clean tea towel and squeeze out any excess moisture.

Blitz the onion, chickpeas and garlic in a food processor until finely chopped.

Tip into a bowl and mix with the sweet potato and seasoning. Mould the mixture into equally shaped thin patties.

Heat the oil in a pan and fry the patties for 8 minutes or until golden. Turn over and cook the other side. Drain on kitchen paper and serve sprinkled with pistachios.

Potato and Chorizo Tortilla

Serves: **6** Preparation time: **20 minutes** Cooking time: **35 minutes**

Ingredients

2 tbsp olive oil

1 onion, peeled and finely sliced

2 large floury potatoes, peeled and diced

100 g / 3 ½ oz / ½ cup chorizo, sliced

1 clove of garlic, crushed

8 eggs

1 tbsp crème fraîche

olive oil

salt and pepper

Method

Preheat the oven to 190°C (170° fan) / 375F / gas 5.

Heat the oil in a pan and gently fry the onion until golden and soft.

Add the potatoes, chorizo and garlic and fry for a few minutes until the fat runs and the potatoes are tender.

Beat the eggs with the crème fraîche in a large bowl.

Add the potato mixture and season then mix together carefully.

Oil a large frying pan, then pour the mixture in and bake for about 35 minutes until puffed and golden. The egg should be cooked through.

Cut into squares and serve warm or cold.

33

Potato Herb Cakes with Red Peppers

Serves: **4** Preparation time: **20 minutes** Cooking time: **15-20 minutes**

Ingredients

1 tbsp butter

1 red pepper, deseeded and finely diced

1 kg / 2 lb / 4 cups cooked potatoes

2 tbsp butter

salt and pepper

½ bunch parsley or coriander (cilantro), chopped

2 tbsp plain (all purpose) flour, seasoned

groundnut oil

tomato salsa, to serve

Method

Heat the butter in a pan and cook the pepper gently until completely softened.

Mash the potatoes thoroughly with the butter, salt and pepper until completely smooth. Mix with the peppers and herbs and shape into patties.

Dust both sides with seasoned flour.

Heat a thin film of oil in a pan and cook the potato cakes 2 at a time until golden and crisp on both sides, adding more oil as necessary.

Serve hot with the tomato salsa.

Broccoli, Tomato and Potato Muffins

Makes: **12** Preparation time: **20 minutes** Cooking time: **25 minutes**

Ingredients

2 eggs, separated

750 g / 1 ⅓ lb / 3 cups floury potatoes, peeled and grated

1 onion, peeled and finely chopped

1 head of broccoli, cut into small florets

12 cherry tomatoes, quartered

100 g / 3 ½ oz / ½ cup plain (all purpose) flour

1 tsp baking powder

salt and pepper

Method

Preheat the oven to 200°C (180° fan) / 400F / gas 6.

Mix the egg yolks with the grated potato, onion, broccoli and tomatoes, flour, baking powder and salt and pepper.

Whisk the egg whites to stiff peaks, then, using a metal spoon, fold into the potato mixture.

Divide the mixture equally, spooning into a greased muffin tin. Bake in the oven for about 25 minutes or until golden.

Turn out and leave to cool for 10 minutes before eating.

Potato and Bacon Breakfast Salad

Serves: **4** Preparation time: **15 minutes** Cooking time: **20-30 minutes**

Ingredients

2 tbsp olive oil

1 tbsp butter

4 large floury potatoes, each sliced into 4 thick rounds

salt and pepper

8 rashers smoked streaky bacon

150 g / 5 oz / ⅔ cup strong Cheddar cheese

16 cherry tomatoes, halved

rocket leaves

Method

Heat the oil and butter in a pan and gently cook the potato rounds in batches until golden and tender all the way through. Alternatively, you could roast them in a hot oven for 20 minutes.

Place 2 bacon rashers slightly overlapping on the surface and place a hunk of cheese at one end. Roll up the bacon to enclose the cheese. Repeat until all bacon is used.

Fry in a pan with a little oil, turning once golden and crisp. Remove and drain on kitchen paper.

Serve the bacon rolls on the potato rounds and garnish with tomatoes and rocket.

Potato and Red Pepper Frittata Canapés

Makes: **24** Preparation time: **15 minutes** Cooking time: **35 minutes**

Ingredients

2 large floury potatoes, peeled and diced

8 eggs

1 tbsp crème fraîche

3 red peppers, seeded and roughly chopped

olive oil

salt and pepper

1 lime, juiced

1 tsp sesame oil

Method

Preheat the oven to 180°C (160° fan) / 350F / gas 4.

Steam the potatoes over simmering water for about 5-7 minutes until tender to the point of a knife.

Sauté the peppers in olive oil until tender.

Beat the eggs with the crème fraîche in a large bowl.

Add the potatoes and season, then add peppers and mix together carefully.

Oil a large frying pan, then pour in the mixture and bake in the oven for about 35 minutes until puffed and golden. The egg should be cooked through.

Cut the frittata into small squares and skewer with toothpicks to serve.

Sweet Potato with Smoked Salmon

Serves: **4** Preparation time: **15 minutes** Cooking time: **15-20 minutes**

Ingredients

2 large sweet
potatoes, peeled

1 onion, peeled and
very finely chopped

salt and pepper

3 tbsp olive oil

4 slices of
smoked salmon

2 tbsp walnuts,
finely chopped

mache salad

Method

Grate the sweet potatoes then tip into a clean tea towel to
squeeze out any excess moisture.

Tip into a bowl and mix with the onion and seasoning.

Mould the mixture into equally shaped thin sausage-shaped
patties.

Heat the oil in a pan and fry the patties for 8 minutes or until
golden, turning occasionally until golden on all sides.

Drain on kitchen paper then wrap each one in a slice of
smoked salmon. Garnish with walnuts and mache salad.

Potato and Sage Croquettes

Serves: **4** Preparation time: **30 minutes** Cooking time: **40 minutes**

Ingredients

1.5 kg / 3 lb / 6 cups floury potatoes, peeled and quartered

50 g / 1 ⅔ oz butter

4 egg yolks, beaten

salt and pepper

¼ bunch sage leaves, finely chopped

6 tbsp flour

2 eggs, beaten

200 g / 7 oz / ¾ cup breadcrumbs, to coat

vegetable oil

Method

Cook the potatoes in boiling salted water until quite tender – about 20 minutes.

Drain thoroughly, then return to the pan and allow to dry briefly over a low heat.

Push the potatoes through a sieve, then add the butter. Work in the egg yolks with a fork, then season and add the sage leaves. Spread the purée in a greased dish and leave to cool.

Lightly flour your hands, then work the cooled mixture into a ball. Shape into a long cylinder and cut into 5 cm logs.

Dip each croquette into the flour, egg and then the breadcrumbs to coat.

Heat the oil to 180°C / 350F.

Deep fry the croquettes in batches for 3-4 minutes until golden-brown. Drain on kitchen paper and serve hot.

Sausage-Stuffed Jacket Potatoes

Serves: **4** Preparation time: **10 minutes** Cooking time: **1 - 1 ½ hours**

Ingredients

4 large baking
potatoes

1 tbsp olive oil

salt and pepper

2 tbsp olive oil

4 Cumberland
sausages

1 onion, peeled and
finely chopped

½ bunch parsley, finely
chopped

Method

Preheat the oven to 200°C (180° fan) / 400F / gas 6.

Rub the potatoes with oil, sprinkle generously with salt and
bake in the oven for 1 - 1½ hours until cooked all the
way through.

Meanwhile slit the sausage skins and take out the meat.

Heat the oil in a pan and cook the crumbled sausage meat
and onions until golden. Season and stir through the parsley.

When the potatoes are cooked, cut in half and scoop out the
flesh, Mix with the sausage mixture then spoon back into the
skins and bake for 10 minutes or until heated through and
crispy on top.

46

Curried Sweet Potato Turnovers

Serves: **8** Preparation time: **30 minutes** Cooking time: **20 minutes**

Ingredients

For the filling:

500 g / 1 lb / 2 cups sweet potatoes, peeled and cubed

1 tbsp olive oil

1 onion, peeled and finely chopped

salt and pepper

pinch cayenne pepper

1 tsp curry powder

500 g / 1 lb ready-rolled puff pastry

1 egg, beaten

2 tbsp pumpkin seeds

Method

Preheat the oven to 200°C (180° fan) / 400F / gas 6.

Cook the potatoes in boiling salted water until tender. Drain thoroughly, then lightly mash.

Cook the onion in oil in a pan until translucent, then add to the crushed potatoes with the spices and seasoning.

Roll the pastry onto a lightly floured surface to about 1cm thickness and cut out eight circles about 10 cm wide.

Spread a little vegetable mixture into the centre of each circle. Brush the edges with a little beaten egg and fold the pastry over to enclose the filling. Using a fork, crimp the edges of the pastry together and brush the parcels with beaten egg. Sprinkle with pumpkin seeds.

Bake in the oven for 10 minutes, then lower the oven temperature to 180°C (160° fan) / 350F / gas 4 and cook for 10 minutes until puffed and golden.

Potato, Ham and Basil Tart

Serves: **4** Preparation time: **15 minutes** Cooking time: **20-30 minutes**

Ingredients

375 g / 13 oz ready-rolled shortcrust pastry

400 g / 14 oz / 1 ½ cups potatoes, cooked and mashed

75 ml / 2 ½ fl. oz / ⅓ cup milk

75 ml / 2 ½ fl. oz / ⅓ cup butter

100 g / 3 ½ oz / ½ cup Parmesan cheese, grated

4 slices Parma or Serrano ham, shredded

½ bunch basil leaves

salt and pepper

Method

Preheat the oven to 180°C (160° fan) / 350F / gas 4.

Roll the pastry out onto a floured surface and cut out 4 circles large enough to fit individual tartlet cases. Press the pastry into the cases and bake for 10-15 minutes until pale gold. Leave to cool.

Meanwhile gently heat the mashed potato and check the consistency and seasoning. Add milk and butter to make a very smooth spoonable puree, then season to taste. Stir through the cheese.

Once the tart cases have cooled, divide the mashed potato between the cases and use a palette knife to even the surface. Top with ham and return to the oven for a further 15-20 minutes until the cases are deep gold and crisp.

Serve warm and top with fresh basil leaves.

Potato and Haddock Pies

Serves: 4 Preparation time: **40 minutes** Cooking time: **20-25 minutes**

Ingredients

400 g / 14 oz
smoked haddock

400 ml / 14 fl. oz / 1 ½
cups milk

6 black peppercorns

1 bay leaf

4 potatoes, peeled
and diced

40 g / 1 oz butter

1 onion, finely chopped

1 stick celery, finely sliced

1 ½ tbsp plain flour

salt and pepper

375 g / 13 oz puff pastry

Method

Preheat the oven to 190°C (170° fan) / 375F / gas 5.

Place the haddock in a pan with the peppercorns and bay leaf, cover with milk and simmer for 15 minutes. Leave to cool, then lift out the fish and seasonings, reserving the milk.

Cook the potatoes in boiling salted water until tender. Drain thoroughly.

Heat the butter in a pan, cook the onion and celery, then whisk in the flour. Whisk in the haddock cooking liquor a little at a time to make a thick smooth sauce. Leave to simmer gently for 10 minutes.

Stir the flaked fish and potatoes into the sauce, then season to taste. Pour into 4 individual pie dishes.

Roll the pastry onto a floured surface and cut out 4 circles to cover the pie dishes. Lay them over the filling, cut a small cross in the top, place the pie dishes on a baking sheet and bake for 20-25 minutes until golden and bubbling.

Serve immediately.

Sides

Truffle Mashed Potato

Serves: **4** Preparation time: **15 minutes** Cooking time: **20 minutes**

Ingredients

1 kg / 2 lb / 4 cups floury potatoes, peeled and cut into large chunks

100 ml / 3 ½ fl. oz / ½ cup milk

100 g / 3 ½ oz / ½ cup butter, diced

salt and pepper

½ black truffle, finely chopped OR 1-2 tsp of truffle oil

Method

Cook the potatoes in boiling salted water until tender to the point of a knife.

Drain and dry over the heat briefly to drive off any excess water.

Warm the milk in a pan.

Mash the potatoes with a potato ricer for preference or with a hand-held masher until smooth, whisking in the milk and butter as you go.

Season generously and stir in the truffle, tasting to get the balance to your liking.

Serve hot.

Potatoes with Cinnamon and Raisins

Serves: **4** Preparation time: **5 minutes** Cooking time: **15-20 minutes**

Ingredients

500 g / 1 lb / 2 cups
new potatoes

100 g / 3 ½ oz / ½ cup
raisins, soaked in
hot water

100 g / 3 ½ oz /
½ cup honey

2 tbsp vegetable oil

1 tsp ground
cinnamon

thyme sprigs

Method

Cook the potatoes in boiling salted water until tender to the point of a knife - about 15-20 minutes. Drain.

Mix together the raisins, honey and vegetable oil and toss the potatoes in the dressing and sprinkle over the cinnamon.

Toss with the raisins and garnish with thyme sprigs.

Pea and Turnip Mashed Potatoes

Serves: **4** Preparation time: **20 minutes** Cooking time: **20-25 minutes**

Ingredients

500 g / 1 lb / 2 cups
floury potatoes, peeled
and cut into chunks

2 large turnips, peeled
and cut into chunks

250 g / 9 oz /
1 cup peas

60 g / 2 oz /
¼ cup butter

75 ml / 2 ½ fl. oz /
⅓ cup milk, warmed

salt and pepper

200 g / 7 oz / ¾ cup
firm tofu, diced

Method

Cook the potatoes and turnips in boiling salted water for 15 minutes, then add the peas for the last 5 minutes of cooking.

Drain, ensuring the potatoes and turnips are tender. Return to the heat briefly to drive off any excess water.

Mash thoroughly with a potato ricer or hand-held masher, whisking in the butter and milk, then season well.

Serve hot topped with the diced tofu.

New Potato and Sausage Salad

Serves: **4** Preparation time: **5 minutes** Cooking time: **15-20 minutes**

Ingredients

500 g / 1 lb / 2 cups
new potatoes

2 tbsp vegetable oil

250 g / 9 oz / 1 cup
smoked sausage, sliced

1 tbsp Dijon mustard

2 tbsp red wine vinegar

salt and pepper

4 tbsp extra virgin
olive oil

4 gherkins (cornichons),
sliced lengthways

½ bunch dill, chopped

Method

Cook the potatoes in boiling salted water until tender to the point of a knife.

Meanwhile heat the oil in a pan and cook the sausages until golden and sticky. Whisk together the mustard, vinegar and seasoning, then whisk in the oil to a thick consistency.

Drain the potatoes, then while still hot slice thickly. Toss in the mustard dressing and add the sausages.

Serve hot, garnished with the gherkin slices, dill and a sprinkling of salt and pepper.

Sweet Potatoes with Honey and Raisins

Serves: **4** Preparation time: **15 minutes** Cooking time: **4 ½ hours**

Ingredients

55 ml / 2 fl. oz / 1/4 cup olive oil

900 g / 2 lb / 6 cups sweet potatoes, peeled and diced

110 ml / 4 fl. oz / 1/2 cup honey

100 g / 4 oz / 1/2 cup golden raisins

1 tsp cloves

salt and pepper

sprigs of coriander (cilantro)

Method

Whisk together the olive oil and honey in a small mixing bowl. Coat the sweet potato in the honey and oil mixture and season generously.

Place in a slow cooker and cover with a lid. Cook on a medium setting for 4 hours until tender.

Remove from the slow cooker and arrange in a roasting tray along with the cloves and raisins.

Preheat the oven to 200°C (180°C fan) / 400°F / gas 6. Roast the sweet potatoes for 20 minutes until coloured and golden at the edges.

Remove from the oven and season a little more before spooning into serving dishes. Garnish with the coriander before serving.

Indian-Spiced Potatoes

Serves: **4** Preparation time: **10 minutes** Cooking time: **15 minutes**

Ingredients

2 tbsp groundnut oil

1 tbsp mustard seeds

500 g / 1 lb / 2 cups
potatoes, peeled and diced

½ tsp turmeric

½ red chilli (chili),
deseeded and finely diced

½ tbsp ground cumin

½ tbsp ground coriander

1 glass of water or
vegetable stock

½ bunch fresh coriander
(cilantro), chopped

salt and pepper

½ lemon, juiced

Method

Heat the oil in a large pan and add the mustard seeds.
Cook for 30 seconds until they start to pop.

Tip in the potatoes and the spices and a glass of water or
vegetable stock.

Cover with a lid and cook gently for 10-15 minutes until
the potatoes are tender. Stir every now and then to
prevent sticking.

To serve, season and sprinkle over the coriander and
lemon juice.

Pan-Fried Potatoes with Tomatoes

Serves: **4** Preparation time: **10 minutes** Cooking time: **25-30 minutes**

Ingredients

3 tbsp olive oil

500 g / 1 lb / 2 cups waxy potatoes, halved

4 ripe vine tomatoes, halved

4 sprigs thyme

1 tsp garam masala

salt and pepper

¼ bunch coriander (cilantro), chopped

100 g / 3 ½ oz / ½ cup goats' cheese, sliced

Method

Heat the oil in a pan and sauté the potatoes gently for 10-15 minutes until slightly golden.

Add the tomatoes, thyme, garam masala and seasoning and cook for another 10-15 minutes until the potatoes are tender and the tomatoes have softened.

Stir through the coriander, turn off the heat, then top with slices of cheese. Leave the cheese to melt, then serve in bowls.

Stuffed Country Potatoes

Serves: **4** Preparation time: **10 minutes** Cooking time: **1 - 1 ½ hours**

Ingredients

4 large baking
potatoes

1 tbsp olive oil

salt and pepper

2 tbsp olive oil

1 red onion, peeled
and finely sliced

1 green pepper,
seeded and finely
chopped

1 red pepper, seeded
and finely chopped

100 g / 3 ½ oz / ½ cup
sun-dried tomatoes,
chopped

Method

Preheat the oven to 200°C (180° fan) / 400F / gas 6.

Rub the potatoes with oil, sprinkle generously with salt and
bake in the oven for 1 - 1½ hours until cooked all the
way through.

Meanwhile heat the oil in a pan and sauté the onion and
peppers until soft and golden. Stir through the tomatoes and
season carefully.

Once the potatoes are cooked, cut them in half and divide the
filling equally between the potatoes. Pop back into the oven
for 5 minutes to heat through before serving.

Spicy Potatoes

Serves: **4** Preparation time: **10 minutes** Cooking time: **15 minutes**

Ingredients

2 tbsp groundnut oil

1 tbsp mustard seeds

1 tbsp black onion seeds

500 g / 1 lb / 2 cups
potatoes, peeled and diced

½ tsp turmeric

½ red chilli (chili),
deseeded and finely diced

1 tbsp garam masala

1 glass of water or
vegetable stock

½ bunch fresh coriander
(cilantro), chopped

salt and pepper

½ lemon, juiced

Method

Heat the oil in a large pan and add the mustard and onion seeds. Cook for 30 seconds until they start to pop.

Tip in the potatoes and the spices and a glass of water or vegetable stock, cover with a lid and cook gently for 10-15 minutes until the potatoes are tender. Stir every now and then to prevent sticking.

To serve, season, sprinkle over the coriander and lemon juice.

Potatoes Stuffed with Cheese and Peppers

Serves: **4** Preparation time: **10 minutes** Cooking time: **1 ½ hours**

Ingredients

4 large baking
potatoes

olive oil

salt and pepper

4 tbsp butter

2 yellow peppers,
deseeded and roughly
chopped

100 g / 3 ½ oz / ½ cup
blue cheese, crumbled

Method

Preheat the oven to 200°C (180° fan) / 400F / gas 6.

Rub the potatoes all over with olive oil and salt then prick
the skins with the point of a knife. Bake in the oven for 1 ½
hours or until soft inside.

Meanwhile cook the peppers in a little oil until tender. Leave
to cool slightly then tip into a bowl with the cheese.

When the potatoes are cooked, cut off the top third and scoop
out the potato flesh, leaving a thick wall to support
the structure.

Mash the potato flesh with the butter, cheese and peppers
then spoon back into the hollowed potatoes.

Return to the oven and bake until the filling is hot and
oozing. Top with the cut off 'hats' and serve.

Potatoes with Fromage Frais and Tomatoes

Serves: **4** Preparation time: **20 minutes** Cooking time: **20-25 minutes**

Ingredients

8 large floury potatoes, peeled and turned

3 ripe vine tomatoes

200 g / 7 oz / ¾ cup fromage frais

½ bunch basil leaves, finely chopped

salt and pepper

2 tbsp extra virgin olive oil.

Method

Hollow out the centre of the potatoes to leave room for the stuffing. Discard the centre.

Steam the potatoes over simmering water until just tender to the point of a knife. Set aside.

Meanwhile blanch the tomatoes in boiling water, then peel off the skins. Dice the flesh, discarding the seeds, and mix with the fromage frais, chopped basil and seasoning. Stir through the extra virgin oil until thick and combined.

Use a spoon to stuff the hollowed-out potatoes and serve sprinkled with basil leaves.

Roast Potatoes
with Mint Sauce

Serves: **4** Preparation time: **10 minutes** Cooking time: **45-50 minutes**

Ingredients

1 kg / 2 lb / 4 cups
new potatoes

2 tbsp olive oil

1 bunch mint leaves,
finely chopped

½ bunch parsley,
chopped

1 clove of garlic,
crushed

200 ml / 7 fl. oz /
¾ cup plain yoghurt

salt and pepper

Method

Preheat the oven to 200°C (180° fan) / 400F / gas 6.

Tip the potatoes into a foil-lined roasting tin and cook in the oven for about 30 minutes, until starting to turn golden.

Whiz the remaining ingredients in a food processor until combined.

Spoon over the potatoes and toss to coat thoroughly. Return to the oven for 20 minutes, until the potatoes are tender.

Serve hot.

Potatoes à la Sarladaise

Serves: **4** Preparation time: **15 minutes** Cooking time: **45-60 minutes**

Ingredients

1 kg / 2 lb / 4 cups waxy potatoes

3 tbsp goose fat

1 bunch parsley, finely chopped

3 cloves of garlic, finely chopped

salt and pepper

Method

Peel the potatoes and slice into thin rounds.

Heat the goose fat in a large pan, then add the potatoes and cook until starting to brown. Lower the heat and cook gently, turning occasionally, until completely tender.

Finely chop the garlic and parsley together to make a persillade, then season with salt and pepper.

Toss the cooked potatoes with the persillade and serve immediately.

Oven-Baked Sweet Potato Chips

Serves: **2** Preparation time: **10 minutes** Cooking time: **30 minutes**

Ingredients

2 sweet potatoes

4 tbsp olive oil

salt and pepper

Method

Preheat the oven to 200°C (180° fan) / 400F / gas 6.

Cut the potatoes into batons and toss with oil and seasoning, then tip onto a baking tray

Roast in the oven for 20-30 minutes, turning once, until golden.

Serve sprinkled with more salt.

Salmon Stuffed New Potatoes

Makes: **12** Preparation time: **10 minutes** Cooking time: **30-40 minutes**

Ingredients

12 small new potatoes

2 tbsp olive oil

salt and pepper

200 g / 7 oz / ¾ cup smoked salmon

2 shallots, finely chopped

12 sun-dried tomato pieces, finely chopped

½ bunch chervil, finely chopped

2 tbsp extra virgin olive oil

Method

Preheat the oven to 200°C (180° fan) / 400F / gas 6.

Rub the potatoes with oil, sprinkle with salt and bake in the oven for about 30-40 minutes until cooked all the way through.

Meanwhile finely dice the salmon, and mix with the shallots, tomatoes, chervil and extra virgin olive oil. Season to taste.

When the potatoes are cooked, cut in half and carefully scoop out 1 tsp of potato. Pile the salmon mix into the hollows and serve.

Dinner
Party

Rosti
Burger Stack

Serves: **4** Preparation time: **20 minutes** Cooking time: **20-25 minutes**

Ingredients

500 g / 1 lb / 2 cups
potatoes, peeled

2 tbsp butter, melted

2 tbsp vegetable oil

salt and pepper

500 g / 1 lb / 2 cups
beef, minced

1 onion, peeled and
grated

1 clove of garlic

1 heaped tbsp grain
mustard (optional)

4 ripe tomatoes,

watercress

Method

Grate the potatoes. Toss with the melted butter and
seasoning, until thoroughly coated. Heat the oil in a large
frying pan, then divide the mixture into 8. Add the mixture in
heaped spoonfuls to the pan, pressing them down flat with a
spatula. Cook over a medium heat for about 10 minutes until
the base is brown.

Run the spatula underneath to loosen, then turn the rosti
over. Cook for a further 5-10 minutes until crisp, then remove
to kitchen paper to drain. Repeat until all the rosti are cooked.

Meanwhile mix the beef thoroughly with the flavourings and
season well. Shape into 4 patties and fry for 3-4 minutes on
either side.

To serve, place a rosti on a plate, add a burger then top with
watercress sprigs and sliced tomato. Finish with a rosti
and serve.

89

Potatoes and Prawns with Gorgonzola Sauce

Serves: **4**   Preparation time: **10 minutes**   Cooking time: **20 minutes**

Ingredients

4 large floury potatoes, peeled

2 tbsp olive oil

16 large shelled prawns (shrimp), raw

300 ml / 10 fl. oz / 1 ¼ cups double (heavy) cream

1 clove of garlic, crushed

100 g / 3 ½ oz / ½ cup Gorgonzola cheese

salt and pepper

Method

Cut the potatoes into very thick slices, so you get 3 thick rounds from each potato. Discard the ends. Steam the rounds over simmering water until tender to the point of a knife - 15 minutes or so.

For the last 5 minutes of cooking, add the prawns and steam until pink and cooked.

Meanwhile heat the cream in a pan with the garlic and cheese until the cheese has melted and the sauce is smooth. Season carefully.

Serve the potato rounds topped with prawns and spoon the sauce over the top.

Spicy Vegetable Curry

Serves: **4** Preparation time: **20 minutes** Cooking time: **30 minutes**

Ingredients

50 ml / 1 ½ fl. oz / ⅕ cup sunflower oil

1 onion, finely chopped

1 tsp black poppy seeds

1 large red chilli (chili), halved

2 cloves of garlic, minced

1 tsp cumin, 1 tsp garam masala

1 tsp coriander, ½ tsp turmeric

½ tsp chilli (chili) powder, 1 bay leaf

500 g / 1 lb / 2 cups potatoes, cubed and boiled

4 carrots, peeled and chopped

curry leaves

300 ml / 10 fl. oz / 1 ¼ cups vegetable stock

Method

Heat the sunflower oil in a large pan and sauté the onion, poppy seeds and chilli until softened and golden.

Add the garlic, all the spices, the bay leaf and 1 tsp of salt and stir well. Cook for 1 minute, then add the potatoes and carrots to the pan.

Add the stock and cook, covered, for 20-25 minutes until the potato is just breaking down.

Serve hot.

93

Prawns and Tomato Confit Mash

Serves: **4** ❦ Preparation time: **20 minutes** ❦ Cooking time: **3 ½ hours**

Ingredients

250 g / ½ lb / 1 cup plum tomatoes

6 cloves of garlic

thyme and rosemary

6 tbsp olive oil

1 kg / 2 lb / 4 cups potatoes, peeled and chopped

100 ml / 3 ½ fl. oz / ½ cup milk

100 g / 3 ½ oz / ½ cup butter

salt and pepper

16 large prawns (shrimps), shelled and raw

sprigs of chervil

Method

Preheat the oven to 130°C (110° fan) / 250F / gas ½.

Halve the tomatoes and place in a roasting tin. Scatter over the garlic and herbs and drizzle with oil. Slow-roast in the oven for 3 hours until shrivelled. Slice them and set aside.

Cook the potatoes in boiling salted water until tender. Drain, then dry briefly over the heat.

Warm the milk in a pan. Mash the potatoes until smooth, whisking in the milk and butter as you go. Season to taste and stir in the chopped tomatoes.

Skewer the prawns and griddle until pink and cooked through. Season.

Serve a spoon of tomato mash on the plate and top with a brochette of prawns and a sprig of chervil.

94

Seafood and Potato Stew

Serves: **4** Preparation time: **15 minutes** Cooking time: **25 minutes**

Ingredients

2 tbsp olive oil

1 onion, peeled and sliced

2 cloves of garlic, sliced

1 red chilli (chili), finely sliced

2 large potatoes, peeled and chopped

2 carrots, peeled and sliced

400 ml / 14 fl. oz / 1 ½ cups fish stock

2 bay leaves

500 g / 1 lb / 2 cups white fish, cut into chunks

16 prawns (shrimps), raw

salt and pepper

½ lemon, juiced

chervil sprigs

Method

Heat the oil in a casserole dish and cook the onion and garlic until pale gold. Add the chilli and cook for 2 minutes.

Add the potatoes, carrots, stock and bay leaves and simmer for 15 minutes.

Add the fish and prawns and simmer for 5 minutes until just cooked, then stir in the seasoning and lemon juice.

Garnish with chervil and serve.

Smoked Haddock and Dill Fishcakes

Serves: **3-4** Preparation time: **40 minutes** Cooking time: **10 minutes**

Ingredients

225 g / 8 oz / 1 cup smoked haddock

350 ml / 12 fl. oz / 1 ½ cups milk

1 bay leaf

225 g / 8 oz / 1 cup mashed potato

½ bunch dill, chopped

squeeze of lemon juice

salt and pepper

3 tbsp plain (all-purpose) flour

1 egg, beaten

200 g / 7 oz / ¾ cup breadcrumbs

vegetable oil

Method

Place the fish in a pan and cover with the milk and bay leaf. Simmer very gently until the fish is just cooked and flakes away - about 8-12 minutes. Remove from the heat and leave to cool.

Flake the fish into a bowl and add the potatoes, dill and seasoning. Use a little of the cooking milk to bind if it seems a bit dry. Chill for 30 minutes.

Form into equal-sized patties, then dip into the flour, egg, then the breadcrumbs.

Heat 1cm depth of oil in a pan and gently fry the fishcakes on both sides in batches until golden and crisp.

Drain on kitchen paper and serve with salad.

Potato and Chickpea Chaat

Serves: **4** Preparation time: **15 minutes** Cooking time: **10 minutes**

Ingredients

500 g / 1 lb / 2 cups canned chickpeas, drained

2 floury potatoes, peeled and diced

½ onion, peeled and finely chopped

½ bunch coriander (cilantro), chopped

1 tbsp chaat masala powder

2-3 tbsp tamarind paste

1 tsp sugar

pinch chilli (chili) powder

4 tbsp plain yoghurt

1 lime, juiced

Method

Steam the diced potato over simmering water until tender to the point of a knife.

Heat the tamarind paste, sugar, lime and chilli in a small pan to dissolve the sugar, thinning out with a little water if it is too thick. Taste - you may want more sugar. Set aside.

Combine the potatoes, chickpeas, onion, coriander and chaat masala and season carefully.

Pile onto individual plates using circle moulds, then drizzle over the tamarind chutney and yoghurt. Top with a little extra coriander.

Potato, Mushroom and Tomato Gratin

Serves: **4-6** Preparation time: **25 minutes** Cooking time: **30-45 minutes**

Ingredients

30 g / 1 oz butter, softened

1 kg / 2 ¼ lb / 4 ¼ cups new potatoes

50 g / 1 ¾ oz butter

250 g / 9 oz / 1 cup chestnut mushrooms

6 tomatoes

2 cloves of garlic, crushed

salt and pepper

½ bunch thyme leaves

50 g / 1 ¾ oz butter

Method

Preheat oven to 180°C (160° fan) / 350F / gas 4.

Use the softened butter to generously grease a large baking dish.

Slice the potatoes as thinly as possible. Cook the mushrooms in the butter until cooked through. Thickly slice the tomatoes and salt lightly - leave for 10 minutes, then pat dry.

Layer half of the potatoes in the base of the baking dish, season and sprinkle with thyme leaves and garlic, then top with the mushrooms and their cooking juices. Layer over the tomato slices, season with more thyme and garlic then top with the remaining potatoes.

Press down lightly and dot with the remaining butter, place on a baking sheet and bake for 30-45 minutes, then check with a skewer to see if the potatoes are tender. If not, return to the oven and check every 10 minutes.

Leave to settle for 5 minutes before serving.

Octopus and Potato Stew

Serves: **4** Preparation time: **15 minutes** Cooking time: **1 hour 15 minutes**

Ingredients

4 tbsp olive oil

3 red onions, peeled and thickly sliced

3 cloves of garlic, finely sliced

1 octopus, cleaned and cut into small pieces

500 g / 1 lb / 2 cups waxy potatoes, halved

300 ml / 10 fl. oz / 1 ¼ cups fish stock

1 tbsp paprika

salt and pepper

1 lemon, juiced

parsley, chopped

Method

Heat the oil in a pan and cook the onions gently for at least 15 minutes until sweet and golden.

Add the garlic, paprika, potatoes, stock and bubble up.

Add the octopus, cover with a lid and leave to simmer gently for at least 1 hour.

Season, squeeze in the lemon juice, add parsley and serve with bread.

Potato Reblochon Soufflé

Serves: **2** Preparation time: **40 minutes** Cooking time: **15-17 minutes**

Ingredients

2 large floury potatoes, peeled

30 g / 1 oz butter, melted

1 tbsp Parmesan cheese, finely grated

4 eggs, separated

50 ml / 1 ¾ fl. oz / ¼ cup milk

½ bunch chives or parsley, finely chopped

salt and pepper

80 g / 2 ½ oz / ⅓ cup Reblochon cheese, sliced into 4 pieces

Method

Preheat the oven to 190°C (170° fan) / 375F / gas 5.

Boil the potatoes whole in a pan and cook until tender - about 20-25 minutes. Drain thoroughly and leave to dry.

Meanwhile coat the insides of 2 ramekins with melted butter and dust with grated Parmesan cheese. Once the potatoes are cool, grate into a bowl.

Whisk the egg yolks with the milk, then stir into the potato and add the chives and seasoning.

Whisk the egg whites to stiff peaks, fold a third of the whites into the potato mix, then fold in the rest, stirring gently.

Spoon the mixture into the ramekins until half-full then place a slice of cheese onto the mixture. Fill the ramekins to the top, then run a thumb around the inner rim to prevent sticking.

Bake in the oven for 15-17 minutes until golden and puffed. Serve immediately.

Sautéed Duck with Potatoes and Lardons

Serves: **4** Preparation time: **10 minutes** Cooking time: **35 minutes**

Ingredients

4 tbsp olive oil or duck or goose fat (see below)

100 g / 3 ½ oz / ½ cup smoked bacon lardons or pancetta, diced

2 cloves of garlic, lightly crushed

rosemary sprigs

1 kg / 2 lb / 4 cups waxy potatoes, sliced

2 confit duck legs, meat removed and shredded (use the fat from the jar)

sea salt

½ bunch parsley, chopped

Method

Heat the fat in a large pan with the garlic. When the scent begins to rise add the potatoes and coat in the hot fat. Add the rosemary.

Turn the heat down to fairly low, cover the pan and cook for 15-20 minutes until the potatoes are golden on one side.

Turn them over, add the duck meat, cover again and cook for a further 10-15 minutes until tender and golden, and the duck is hot.

Serve immediately, sprinkled with sea salt and parsley.

Gratin Dauphinois
with Broccoli

Serves: **4-6** Preparation time: **20 minutes** Cooking time: **1 ½ - 2 hours**

Ingredients

1 head of broccoli, cut into florets

50 g / 1 ¾ oz butter, softened

1 kg / 2 ¼ lb / 4 ¼ cups floury potatoes, peeled

2 cloves of garlic, crushed

salt and pepper

½ bunch thyme

500 ml / 1 pint / 2 cups double (heavy) cream

Method

Preheat oven to 160°C (140° fan) / 325F / gas 3.

Blanch the broccoli florets in boiling salted water for 2 minutes then drain thoroughly and dry on kitchen paper.

Use the softened butter to generously grease a large baking dish.

Slice the potatoes as thinly as possible – about 3 mm, using either a sharp knife or, a mandoline.

Layer the potatoes in the baking dish, season and sprinkle with the broccoli florets, thyme leaves and garlic as you go.

Pour the cream over the potatoes – it should come just to the top of the potatoes.

Push the potatoes down into the cream, place on a baking tray and bake for 1 ½ - 2 hours.

Leave for 5 minutes to settle before serving.

110

Warm Potato, Chicken and Sugarsnap Pea Salad

Serves: **4** Preparation time: **15 minutes** Cooking time: **20-25 minutes**

Ingredients

3 tbsp olive oil

2 chicken breasts

500 g / 1 lb / 2 cups waxy potatoes, halved

100 g / 3 ½ oz / ½ cup sugar snap peas

6 spring onions (scallions), finely chopped

2 handfuls rocket leaves

4 tbsp extra virgin olive oil

salt and pepper

½ lemon, juiced

Method

Preheat the oven to 200°C (180° fan) / 400F / gas 6.

Roast the chicken with a little oil and seasoning for about 20 minutes, until cooked through. Set aside, loosely covered to keep warm.

Meanwhile heat 2 tbsp oil in a pan and sauté the potatoes until golden and tender.

Steam the sugarsnap peas until tender - about 3-4 minutes.

Tip the chicken resting juices into a small bowl and whisk in the extra virgin olive oil, lemon juice and seasoning.

Slice the chicken thickly, then add to a large serving bowl with the potatoes, sugarsnap peas, rocket and spring onions. Use large spoons to toss with the dressing and serve.

Potato and Pancetta Pizza

Serves: **3-4** ❈ Preparation time: **40 minutes** ❈ Cooking time: **8-10 minutes**

Ingredients

For the pizza dough:

400 g / 14 oz / 1 ½ cups white bread flour

100 g / 3 ½ oz / ½ cup semolina flour

½ tbsp salt

1 x 7 g sachet dried yeast

½ tbsp caster (superfine) sugar

350 ml / ½ pint / 1/3 cup lukewarm water

For the topping: Per pizza

6 tbsp passata

4 new potatoes, cooked and sliced

1 tsp thyme leaves

2 tbsp pancetta, cooked

½ ball mozzarella

extra virgin olive oil

black pepper

Method

Pour the flour and salt into a bowl and make a well in the centre. Add the yeast and sugar, mix with a fork and leave for a few minutes. When frothing, pour into the well. Using a fork bring in the flour from around the insides and mix well.

When it starts to come together, use your hands and pat it into a ball.

Knead the dough for 10 minutes until smooth. Flour the dough, cover with film and leave for 30 minutes.

Preheat the oven to 240°C (220° fan) / 475F / gas 9

Flour the surface, tear off a piece of dough and roll into a circle 0.5 cm thick. Dust with a little flour. Cover with film and leave for 30 minutes.

Spread the base with the passata, layer on the potatoes with the thyme. Scatter over the pancetta and lay on the mozzarella slices.

Place in the oven on a baking tray for 8-10 minutes until golden and crisp.

Drizzle with extra virgin olive oil, grind over some pepper and serve hot.

Tuna Marmitako

Serves: **4** Preparation time: **10 minutes** Cooking time: **30-40 minutes**

Ingredients

4 tbsp olive oil

1 onion, peeled and finely sliced

1 green pepper, deseeded and sliced

1 red pepper, deseeded and sliced

400 g / 14 oz new potatoes, quartered

2 cloves of garlic, finely chopped

3 sprigs thyme

150 ml / 5 fl. oz / ⅔ cup white wine

350 g / 12 oz fresh tuna steak, cubed

salt and pepper

Method

Heat the oil in a large shallow pan with a lid and gently fry the onion and peppers until golden.

Add the potatoes, thyme and garlic, toss to coat in the oil, pour in the wine, cover with a lid and leave to simmer for 15 minutes or until the potatoes are tender.

Add the tuna, season and cook until the tuna just turns opaque but remains pink in the middle. Adjust the seasoning and serve with crusty bread.

Layered Potato and Pepper Bake

Serves: **4-6** Preparation time: **20 minutes** Cooking time: **1 ½ hours**

Ingredients

50 g / 1 ¾ oz butter, softened

1 kg / 2 ¼ lb / 4 ¼ cups floury potatoes, peeled

6 red peppers, deseeded and sliced

1 kg / 2 lb / 4 cups spinach leaves

2 cloves of garlic, crushed

salt and pepper

½ bunch thyme

500 ml / 1 pint / 2 cups vegetable stock

100 g / 3 ½ oz / ½ cup Parmesan cheese, grated

Method

Preheat oven to 180°C (160° fan) / 350F / gas 4.

Use the softened butter to generously grease a large baking dish.

Slice the potatoes as thinly as possible. Wilt the spinach in a pan with 2 tbsp water, then squeeze out any excess liquid.

Layer a third of the potatoes in the baking dish, season and sprinkle with thyme leaves and garlic, then top with the spinach. Add another layer of potatoes, then top with the peppers. Finish with a layer of potatoes.

Pour the stock over the potatoes.

Push the potatoes down into the stock, place on a baking tray and bake for 1 ½ hours.

Thirty minutes before the end of cooking, dot the top with the cheese, then continue to cook until golden. Leave for 5 minutes to settle before serving.

Cod and Potato Cheesy Bake

Serves: **4** Preparation time: **25 minutes** Cooking time: **20-25 minutes**

Ingredients

750 g / 1 ⅓ lb / 3 cups new potatoes, thinly sliced

½ bunch chives, finely chopped

salt and pepper

2 heads chicory leaves, finely sliced

400 g / 14 oz cod fillet, cut into 4 equal pieces

60 g / 2 oz / ¼ cup butter, melted

150 g / 5 oz / ⅔ cup Mimolette cheese, grated

Method

Preheat the oven to 190°C (170° fan) / 375F / gas 5.

Layer the potato slices in overlapping rows in the base of 4 individual gratin dishes. Season and sprinkle over the chives. Drizzle with butter.

Top with sliced chicory then top with a cod fillet and season again.

Sprinkle the cheese over the cod and bake in the oven for 20-25 minutes until the potatoes are tender when pierced with a skewer.

Pan-Fried Potatoes and Prawns

Serves: **4** Preparation time: **10 minutes** Cooking time: **25-30 minutes**

Ingredients

4 tbsp olive oil

2 garlic cloves, lightly crushed

2 tbsp cumin seeds

1 kg / 2 lb / 4 cups waxy potatoes, sliced

16 large prawns (shrimps), shell on, raw

sea salt

½ bunch parsley, chopped

1 lemon, juiced

Method

Heat the oil in a large pan with the garlic. When the scent begins to rise add the potatoes and turn to coat in the hot fat. Add the cumin seeds.

Turn the heat down to fairly low, cover the pan and cook for 15-20 minutes until the potatoes are golden on one side.

Turn them over, add the prawns, cover again and cook for a further 10-15 minutes until tender and golden and the prawns are pink.

Serve immediately, sprinkled with sea salt, parsley and drizzled with lemon juice.

Salmon and Potato Soup

Serves: **4** Preparation time: **20 minutes** Cooking time: **25-30 minutes**

Ingredients

50 g / 1 ¾ oz butter

1 small onion, peeled

1 stick celery, finely chopped

1 carrot, peeled

400 g / 14 oz / 1 ½ cups new potatoes

200 ml / 7 fl. oz / ¾ cup fish stock

800 ml / 1 ¾ pints / 3 ⅓ cups milk

1 bay leaf, salt and pepper

350 g / 12 oz / 1 ½ cups salmon fillet, cubed

100 ml / 3 ½ oz / ½ cup double (heavy) cream

2 tbsp parsley

Method

Heat the butter in a pan and sweat the finely chopped onion, diced carrot and celery without colouring.

Add the peeled and sliced potatoes and cook for a few minutes, then pour in the fish stock and milk, add the bay leaf and seasoning and simmer gently for 20 minutes or so until the potatoes are tender.

Add the salmon to the soup and simmer for 5-8 minutes until just cooked.

Add the cream and reheat gently, stir in some finely chopped parsley and serve.

Sautéed Potatoes with Smoked Sausage

Serves: **4** Preparation time: **10 minutes** Cooking time: **20 minutes**

Ingredients

750 g / 1 ¾ lb / 3 ⅓ cups waxy potatoes, scrubbed and sliced

3 tbsp olive oil

salt and pepper

350 g / 12 oz / 1 ½ cups smoked sausage, sliced

½ bunch parsley, chopped

Method

Heat the oil in a pan and sauté the potatoes until golden and cooked through - about 15-20 minutes.

Remove from the pan with a slotted spoon and drain on kitchen paper.

Add the sausage to the pan and cook until golden and starting to crisp. Tip the potatoes back into the pan, season and sprinkle over the parsley. Serve hot.

INDEX